Fine in a Minute

Poems by
King Daddy

BAMBOO DART PRESS

LOS ANGELES † NEW YORK † LONDON † MELBOURNE

Fine in a Minute, poems by King Daddy

978-1-947240-94-0   Paperback

978-1-947240-95-7   eBook

Cover art by Dolly Torres
Edited by Kevin Ausmus
Additional editing and author photo by Joanne Qualey Baines
Layout and design by Mark Givens

"Rubescense" first appeared in *Gynaddiction*, Ballgag Press, 1999

"Fold" first appeared in *Beat Not Beat*, Moontide Press, 2022

For information:

Bamboo Dart Press

chapbooks@bamboodartpress.com

Bamboo Dart Press 047

Pelekinesis
www.pelekinesis.com

BAMBOO DART PRESS
www.bamboodartpress.com

SHRiMPER
www.shrimperrecords.com

For
Wendrika Gael Thorpe
a.k.a. "Betty Nude"
my one true love

CONTENTS

SUMMER DRESS (THE WENDRIKA POEMS)

GONE (GHAZALS)

ACKNOWLEDGMENTS

Heartfelt thanks to -

Betty Nude (RIP), Brutus Chieftain (RIP), Ed Baines (RIP), Miss Mableton Georgia, 1952, Emily Marie Hayes (RIP), Kevin Ausmus, Joanne Q. Baines, Dolly Torres, Poets in Distress, PondWater Society, Bamboo Dart Press, the Thorpe family, the Flores family, the Torres family, the Bender family, Jennifer Bradpiece, Ron Koertge, Raundi Moore-Kondo, Rich Ferguson, Steve Lossing, Jamie Why, Deborah Bogen, Jim Bogen, Julie Lansford, James Achedafty, Lori McGinn, Daniel McGinn, Leo Zulueta, Dianne Mansfield, Robert Jones, Trig, Ace, Fat Tony, Miss Kitty, Bearknuckle Honey, Wilco, the Mountain Goats, Nirvana, Starlite Mobile Estates (space 26), San Onofre State Beach (trail 6), the Los Angeles public library system, and the Buddha.

Sometimes the Meat is Tender

Yesterday, feeling fine

I called in sick to work
had a stiff shot
of Four Roses bourbon
read some Bukowski
masturbated to
lactation/bondage porn
baked a bundt cake
smoked a gang of weed
talked to the dog
about Buddha
listened to a
Blind Lemon Jefferson record
ate ice cream
straight from the carton
took two naps
and wrote this poem

The Moon was Waxing, The Moon was Waning, There was No Moon

it was the burning heart of August
it was the last blue day of May
it was bleak December

it was six ravens perched on
    a driftwood log
it was a pair of boots slung
    over a telephone wire
it was two dozen scattered tamales
    and a ripped paper bag

it was liberty hysteria
it was an approach/avoidance conflict
it was defiance of socio-cultural norms

it was the pout of the never-petted
it was the intractability of desire
it was black cow's milk and black hen's eggs

I lay with my ear to the ground
    and heard faint murmurings
I stood with my head held high
    my gaze piercing
I fell accelerating at a rate of
    32 ft. per second per second

I screamed glory until my throat was raw
I whispered the poems of old Buddhas
     until my tongue was swollen
I spoke not a mumblin' word

she was huge above her stockings
she was a tiny thing in a holey
     Johnny Thunders t-shirt
she was a pear-shaped woman wearing
     red lace panties three sizes too small

she said – just hold me 'til the spinning stops
she said – there's something broken in your eyes
she said – count to three but do it on two

Poems is Hard

poems is unlovely business
poems is barking back at the hellhounds
poems is by my fruits ye shall know me
poems is built up block by block
      knocked down, kicked about
      and built up again
poems is messing around – *no*
      fucking around – *no*
      screwing around with syntax
poems is hours spent adrift in fictive worlds
      absent from the golden present moment
poems is hard

poems is home dentistry
poems is a celibate mistress
poems is blood sweat and tears
      semen snot and vomit
      and tears
poems is the chisel in the crack
      between uselessness and inutility
poems is the wrinkles in a half-deflated
      yellow mylar happy face balloon
poems is a solemn brown-eyed girl whispering
      a burning secret in your ear
poems is hard

poems is love me love me love me
poems is shut up god damn it shut up
poems is a lime green cuddly toy
       with its eyes plucked out and
       awful stains around its mouth
poems is a raggedy November sparrow
       singing in a minor key
poems is six wriggling giveaway kittens
       in a cut-down Huggies box
poems is a shit-colored mule
       standing in the rain

Slump

I was feather
I was riffle
I was cipher
I was wisp

knowing full well
that time comes
rushing on like waves
I pissed away whole days

listening to the drone
of small airplanes
transported
as if by angelic choir

my notebooks were deserts
my pen was filled with sand
the damp tentacles of doubt crept
through my egomind like groundfog

I gathered up a great armful of
I-can't-make-poems
and clutched it to my chest
carried it with me everywhere

learned to favor it silently
like a sore foot
dandled it on my knee
like a giggling grandchild

rode it like a flume ride
jaws clenched
waiting
for the cooling spray

Pondwater Funk

I dreamed of black
wings flapping and woke
cursing crows
another July gone

my head tuned to distant stations
all wild and dire
with compulsion and treasons

I stepped outside
to smoke my breakfast
caught a pondwater funk
on the morning breeze

I found an oily black
pinfeather floating
in my coffee
grim August augury

it tasted dark and steely
like licking a smithy's anvil
I drank it down for maximum
reverberation and haunt

stern focus
deepens what it regards
what I regard must seduce me
or I'll look away

there is only a moment
when something is
going
and then it's gone

this is an old song
these are old blues
a rag a bone
and a hank of hair

I said it once before
but it bears repeating
I've got a great big secret
written down somewhere

rook and raven
magpie and sin
you don't want to see
what the crows dragged in

Little Triggers

yes I know
in the algebra of lifespan
idleness equals loss
yes I know
years ago I promised
someday soon
yes I know
it looks like I left my ass
in my other pants
yes I know
my sound-of-one-hand-clapping
ringtone is ineffective
yes I know
guacamole is extra

little triggers
little triggers
little triggers
I bristle with
little triggers

woeful are the limits of my powers
my mojo is crumbling
tonight no one sits
dreamily doodling "Mrs. Greg Thorpe"

in a spiral notebook
I haven't been kissed on the neck
by anyone who shouldn't be
kissing me on the neck
in 22 months
even the little dog is over me
just stares straight through me
there was a time
she danced and spun at my heels
like a minstrel's bitch

little triggers
little triggers
little triggers
I bristle with
little triggers

do you not see me
standing here
holding this large ball of light
offering it
to each of you
in turn

Prairie Dream

everything is askew
everyone is the wrong age

I am not lonely
my mouth is not broken

the sky is cloudless and vast
the horizons are impossible

in the whitest
cleanest sunlight

Mom and Dad hold hands
"Idn't it pretty, Mama?"

they move across a broad plain
of sedge and scrub

it seems to go on forever
it won't

Papaw walks out ahead
dipping snuff and humming

my unborn grandson
rides on his shoulders

he is surefooted
strides with gentle purpose

carries a schoolmarm's pointer
aims it at things

declaims
ever teaching

I follow at a distance
fall farther and farther behind

stopping to name
every bird I flush

cock pheasant
black phoebe

meadowlark

Fold

call my family
tell them I'm lost
on the sidewalk
no, it's not okay

squint to see it

on a scarred white table
in a dusty mason jar
my last easy breath
she unscrewed the lid

pulled up my shirt
fingernails painted milk white
she soft scratched my back
spelled out Wilco lyrics

until I waved a white flag
she told me to unclench
nobody wanted to be there
nobody wanted to leave

I was driving six white horses
she was spasm and honey
said burn down the house
pulled me into the fold

she

pulled me into the fold
said burn down the house
she was spasm and honey
I was driving six white horses

nobody wanted to leave
nobody wanted to be there
she told me to unclench
until I waved a white flag

spelled out Wilco lyrics
she soft scratched my back
fingernails painted milk white
pulled up my shirt

she unscrewed the lid
my last easy breath
in a dusty mason jar
on a scarred white table

squint to see it

no, it's not okay
on the sidewalk
tell them I'm lost
call my family

Tender

sometimes
the meat is tender

sometimes
the stairs are scattered
with broken glass

sometimes
they smoke cigarettes
on the porch
while the sky goes pretty

sometimes
they take up knives
and roam the neighborhood
carve their initials
into separate trees

sometimes
they drink their pockets empty
dance a raggedy dance
can't find their footing
but the falling
hardens their bodies

sometimes
he hews to his principles
remembers where he comes from
and what he carries

sometimes
his eyes turn to fists
and the silence
creeps over him

sometimes
she finds scraps of paper
in his pockets
clamps them to her temples
steals light like the moon

sometimes
she flees to the backyard
hunches on a ruptured
brick wall
scratches mute curses
in the dirt

sometimes
they hold late night
80 proof talk talk talks
like bayou graveyards
nothing stays buried

sometimes
orphaned by their mother tongue
they retreat to their neutral corners
and mutter in dead languages

sometimes
they chase lucidity
test drive different vehicles
St. John's wort, mushrooms, threesomes

sometimes
he gentles up to
the manger she sleeps in
whispers confessions
to sins of omission

sometimes
panicked and wracked
she puts her hands on him
searches his chest for treasure

sometimes
they put a dry kettle
on the stove
pull up chairs
and wait for the whistle

sometimes
in the whiskey dark
they lean into one another
belly up and bear down
until someone cries uncle

sometimes
aroused and indicted
they throw open the windows
and cringe at the light

sometimes
black pearls to platinum
in the sun
tests the timbre
of their hearts

sometimes
there is gentle gesture
and slick friction

sometimes
brute fidelity
and dark barter

sometimes
only guillotine
and gravity

Poor Shepherd

I've been a poor shepherd to my flock
there are wolves in the fold

I've been drunk since my mom got sick
and her gone all these years

I've been sick since I lost my grip
sunk below my raising

I've been lost since my girl took off
just bottled up and bailed

I've been handed riches and wonders
and pissed them all away

from the south hills of Covina
my father's ghost stares down at me

ashen

This is Not a Cry for Help

Rubescence

the first time it happens
he hurries to the bathroom
drops his pants and finds
his boxer shorts soaked
with blood
the crotch of his jeans
stained startling red
there is no pain
and he can't tell
where the blood is coming from

he cleans up
then looks in the mirror
he sees a crimson
trail running
from his left ear

if he stands in one place
too long
he leaves scarlet footprints
so he keeps moving

often he finds
his palms suddenly bloody
if the kids are around

he shoves his hands
quickly into his pockets
so they won't notice
but kids see everything

he doesn't say anything
to the wife
but she washes his clothes
she's got to know by now

there are never any
tangible wounds
no pain
he knows it's not
some religious crap
never touches the stuff
and he knows somehow
that it's not medical

so he carries
pre-moistened towelettes
and starts wearing dark clothes
better to hide the stains
and boots are good
they catch all the blood
that run down his legs
though the sloshing is vulgar

finally
he's so drawn
pale listless
they confront him
Honey Dad
what's with all the blood

he wants to tell
them that he doesn't know
is dying to know
but when he opens
his mouth to speak
a red-black wave
washes down his chin
and onto this piece of paper

Fine in a Minute

maybe all of this shouldn't bother me
like it does, but it does
neuroscience has shown us
that neither colors nor sounds
exist outside of our brains
furthermore
I have come to understand
that all matter is merely energy
condensed to a slow vibration
that we are made up of stardust
and literally contain the universe
that our bodies are miraculous machines
of phenomenal complexity
made up of multiple trillions of molecules
each vibrating with its own intelligence
and don't you ever wonder if
that light at the end of the tunnel
as we are dying thing
is nothing more than us being pushed
through another birth canal

I'll be fine in a minute

I spend all my writing sessions
confessing transgressions

and striking them out
I try to take seriously
acts of language
try to write myself right
not because I want to say something
but because I have something to say
I don't make friends with my writing
it is slightly out of my control
you, the reader, play no part here
this is a private matter
there are poems in me
that paper can't handle
polished gems of observation
shining and diamond hard
but I kill them in their cribs
slash precise lies into my notebooks
foregoing all truth and beauty
and give voice to monsters

I'll be fine in a minute

shed the night, grind the coffee
get behind the mule
I've done 30 years at the same job
and I'm not sure
if I can do 30 more days
when my shift is over
I take off my shoes in the parking lot

and clap them together like chalk erasers
so I don't carry one speck
of that mess home with me
I think it's time for a career change
I am studying to be a deacon in the
Church of the Disembodied Spirit of Kurt Cobain
it's a flickering torch, but I'm carrying it
if that doesn't pan out
I've procured an old felt hat
and a dented tin cup
and crafted a cardboard sign reading -
MY MOTHER LOVED ME
BUT NOW SHE'S GONE

I'll be fine in a minute

sometimes I feel like a man
trapped in a man's body
beneath this well-rendered surface
beats a heart brilliant with confusion
I have ironclad scruples
and a willingness to violate them
my heart engages in acts
that my head stands against
clearly the heart is wild
and yearns to be free
that's why our ribs are cages
the heart is not a metaphor

no wait, the heart *is* a metaphor
my heart is a brightly fletched arrow
trembling in its rest as the tension
of the bowstring grows too great to bear
no, my heart is a smoky gray village
with a cackling raven chained to a post
in the main square
no, yes, my heart is a cackling raven

I'll be fine in a minute

oh the cold weight of the crown
I don't know if it's Tuesday or Shreveport
everyone answers my texts with WTF
what the fuck does WTF mean
I've been taking the wrong dreams
to bed with me at night
the fan in my room
sounds like someone crying
so I turn up the radio
and the next three songs make me cry
I search all 1200 sq. ft. of the house
for my wife and find her
at the kitchen table, crying
counting the beads
on her abacus of disappointment
she tells me we have forsworn our dreams
sometimes I don't know I'm crying until

I notice my terrier bitch dancing at my heels
what am I crying about
I have a library and a garden

I'll be fine in a minute

I've been trying to be where I am
to be stubbornly interested
in the present moment
not to reconstruct what has just happened
I've tried sitting with mindfulness
quietly still
and knowing my breath
but I can't seem to
hold onto my herenowness
I've made some strides lately
for whole minutes at a time
I've been able to maintain the insight
of nonself and lovingkindness
I've been making demo tapes
of the new me
but everyone seems to like
my old stuff better
I've interacted with 17 people today
and not one of them recognized me
as the Buddha

I'll be fine in a minute

I was half a country away
when my Papaw died
unable to get home
as he was conveyed to his resting place
I left my post
and sat alone in the barracks
trying to feel the weight
of one-sixth of a coffin
I shared a Dr. Pepper with my Granny
on her 84th birthday
perched on the edge of her hospital bed
when she died early that evening
I was outside smoking
the night before we buried my Dad
I flicked lint from his collar
as he lay in his casket
and told him some things
I should have told him sooner
I tried to talk to my Mom at the very end
as she was born away on show white wings
but found myself singing an Appalachian spiritual
because when I forget how to talk
I sing
and when I forget how to sing
I mumble

I'll be fine in a minute

Tacos de Pescado

I saw Buddha at Señor Baja. Not just any Buddha, *the* Buddha, Siddhartha Gautama, the Awakened One. I knew it was him from his coarse robe and the light seeping out from around the edges of it.

I got my tacos and sat down across from him. "Sid," I said, "it's such an honor to meet you." I saw that he was eating potato tacos and quickly looked down at my fish tacos. "No worries," said the Buddha, "St. Kurt said it's okay to eat fish 'cuz they don't have any feelings." Lovingkindness flowed off of him in waves. I felt caressed.

I told him, "I want to be more like you. I want to walk the path. I want to stop thinking so much, stop burdening my heart with judgments. I want to see clearly the miracle of a single flower."

The Buddha tore open a small paper packet of salt. He sprinkled some on a slice of radish. He looked at it carefully, bit into it and chewed slowly. Naked surfers and great flocks of springtime swallows soared and dipped in his eyes.

"Want, want, want." said the Buddha, "Stop talking. Eat your tacos."

Tammy Doesn't Like Me Anymore

Around 1980 I am at the Foothill Drive-In with
        Heather Welch in the back seat of a day-glo
        orange AMC Gremlin. Her rust-colored dittos
        and my navy OP cord shorts are crumpled on
        the floorboard next to an empty bottle of
        Boone's Farm. The windows are fogged up.
        I have still never seen *Private Benjamin*.

Around 1978 I am at the Troubador. The Weirdos
        are onstage playing "Helium Bar." I grasp
        the concept of cacophony. From this moment
        forward I will actively seek cacophony.

Around 1966 my cat Ringo gets pancaked by the
        Helms Bakery truck. I grasp the concept
        of death and decide to kill Heather Welch,
        my neighborhood nemesis. She is always
        trying to kiss me.

Around 1970 Mom and Dad take the family to the
        Foothill Drive-In to see *A Man Called Horse*.
        When the Lakota pierce the British guy
        through the chest and suspend him by
        leather straps, I scrunch up next to Mom

and hide my eyes. The Brit endures the tribe's torturous ritual and goes on to become chief. I am hazardously happy.

Around 1995 I am in a very white room in West Hollywood. I pay a man to push large needles through my nipples and insert jewelry. A Led Zeppelin song that I haven't heard for 15 years is playing. I am hazardously happy.

Around 2012 I try, but fail, to form the Topless Tuesday Pancake Dinner Club.

Around 2018 my one true love succumbs to her demons. Alcoholic liver failure, at 47. I will never walk the same again.

Around 1974 I am walking home with Tammy Davis after school, but during puberty. We stop under a tree and stand very close. I take this as a sign. As soon as our lips touch I force my tongue into her mouth, make guttural noises, tangle my fingers in her hair. The next day at school Stacey tells me Tammy doesn't like me anymore.

Around 2009 I am led to a pond. It ripples with life. It is surrounded with birds and love and genius. I will never stray far from this pond.

Around 1988 I am at the Troubador. Jane's
Addiction is onstage playing "Pigs in Zen."
A big girl in a white leather halter top
and matching miniskirt grabs me by both
wrists and looks into my eyes. She is
sweaty and beautiful. She says, "I've been
brushed by the wingtips of the butterfly
of glory." When I don't reply, she asks
"Do you want to go to Oki Dog?"

Around 1985 I become a father. It's good shit.
I do it again the next year.

Around 2008 I become a grandfather. It's good
shit. I do it over and over in the ensuing
years.

Around 1987 I meet my one true love. She is
wearing 12-hole Doc Martens, a black
petticoat and bustier, and far too many
bracelets. She has Robert Smith hair.
Her eyes are rimmed with kohl. They
are sea green with tiny flecks of
cornflower blue and buckwheat. My wife
hates her. I realize instantly that, like
Picasso needed paint, like Hendrix needed
feedback, I will need her at my reach. I shrug
off the wife and spend the next 30 years with her.

Around 2001, on an immaculate summer afternoon, on
a deserted stretch of wilderness beach, I
stroll naked on the edge of the
continent. I briefly understand everything.

Around 2019 I am at the Troubador. Lost Dog
Street Band is onstage playing "September
Doves." My daughter and granddaughter, pushed
up against the front of the stage, turn and
beckon me forward. I squirm my way
to them.

Around 1985 I get booted out of the Air Force
for smokin' them left-handed cigarettes.

Around 1997 my poetry teacher asks, "what
is duck butter?"

Around 1986 I am in a darkened suburban living
room. The party is over. The guests have
all gone. I examine my system and find
it in need of repairs.

Around 2021 my muses come to me in the night,
slip rings set with precious stones onto
my toes. I kick them off in my sleep.

Wallet Chain Revival

I asked the poem
what it wanted to be
the poem said
I want to be
an attention-seeking missile
I want to be
the Alpha and the Omega
the match and the striker
el clavo y la cruz
I want to be
as clever as
Brutus Chieftain on mead
as haunting as
Lemuel Turner's "Way Down Yonder Blues"
I want to be
a freckled Nebraska transplant
round of ass
and dimpled of cheek
fresh off the bus
bopping down the Hollywood Walk of Fame
in a chrome yellow sundress

I asked the poem
where it wanted to go
the poem said
I want to go
to the Mt. Baldy Zen Center
be still for a week
find my breath
and follow it
I want to go
to the Venice Beach drum circle
sit criss cross applesauce in the sand
while a hirsute hippie girl
named Smash the System
braids my hair
I want to go
to the original Original Tommy's
at Rampart and Beverly
at one in the morning
and with ringing ears
hold a debriefing
on the Skinny Puppy show
at the Palladium
I want to go
to Glendora
see that Debbie girl

I asked the poem
what it wanted to do
the poem said
I want to shake shit up
I want to raise your hackles
align your chakras
shape your sensibilities
I want to start a band
called Wallet Chain Revival
with Bob Jones on guitar
Raundi on bass
and Barack Obama on drums
I want to sit on the porch
on a Summer Thursday
around sundown
talk story and smoke cigarettes
while the sky goes pretty
I want to stalk
the streets of Covina
in a tattered robe
and crooked crown
proclaiming my glory

I asked
and the poem said
I want to find three oranges
and juggle

Manicure

After paying $1,500 cash in advance and waiting six weeks for an appointment with Lucille herself, she arrived at Lucille's Institute of Nailology on Garey Ave. in Pomona with a great sense of anticipation.

Leaving, seven hours later, she surveyed Lucille's handiwork.

Her left pinkie fingernail was painted a rich, pearlescent blue with shimmering silver threads near the borders.

Her left ring fingernail was all saturated primary colors, a simple American flag set against a yellow background. If she put it very close to her ear she could hear Woody Guthrie singing a faint rendition of "This Land is Your Land."

Her left middle fingernail had received only a buff and clear coat. Near the tip a hole was drilled, and from it dangled a tiny charm, cast in pewter, that depicted Mario Savio on the steps of Sproul Hall in December 1964, exhorting the Berkeleyites to action. He is frozen in the moment just before he says, *"...you've got to put your bodies upon the gears, the wheels, upon the levers, upon all the apparatus, and you've got to make it stop."*

Her left index fingernail contained the entire text of "Beowulf," applied with a brush whose single bristle was crafted from one of Lucille's own eyelashes.

Her left thumbnail had carved into it an impression of Jonathan Livingston Seagull. In the sunlight, the crystalline precision and economy of line took her breath away.

Her right thumbnail appeared unadorned but for a smudge of what could have been storm clouds near the tip. As she studied it, Jonathan flapped his wings twice and flew over from her left thumb as heavy raindrops began to fall.

Her right index fingernail had, atop a lurid pink base coat, a head-and-shoulders portrait of Memphis bluesman Furry Lewis with a text balloon above his head, reading, "The best place to pick up women is the canned mackerel section of the Piggly Wiggly."

Her right middle fingernail was removed entirely and replaced with a 1976 Roosevelt dime, firmly affixed with surgical Super Glue.

Her right ring fingernail had a photorealistic representation of Desperation Squad lead singer Mr. P wearing only beat-down running shoes, a graying athletic supporter and a shabby panda head. It was an amazing likeness, he appeared completely unmoored. As she applied the finishing touches, Lucille had said, "Honey, this man is a hometown hero. Don't look askance."

Her right pinkie fingernail was painted red.

Right in the Heart

I checked out a book of poems
from Covina Library
a volume of Bukowski's
posthumously published work
in a trade paperback edition

when I got home
I noticed someone had
gotten stabby with it
four knife wounds
marred its glossy cover

the shallowest
(I think of it
as the first)
penetrated only
a few pages deep
to the title page
'The Flash of Lightning Behind the Mountain'

a more substantial wound
made it to page 47
marking a poem
about a horse
dying ugly

on a racetrack
beneath the smog-choked
San Gabriels

another stopped at
page 63
highlighting the line
'*reached into my mouth and plucked rotten teeth*'

the deepest gash
a shanking
plunged all the way
to page 121
leaving just the
slightest dimple
right in the heart
of the middle letter
of the word
'*whore*'

Drowning at the Liquor Store

they say
when you find a feather
you know
you are on the right path
I've never found a feather
I am wayfaring
and recently wrecked
I am ragged
rotten and rent
unraveling

O grant me
sweet absolution for the more unholy
things I've done
then trash the casserole
and soak the pan
take my picture
off the wall
strike the match
burn down the house

I have spent
the bright coins
of my youth
I have no motor

and no rudder
the dream
is in the ditch
my heart is a porcupine
my mouth is a minefield
my braids are all split-endy

my floor and my phone
are flooded
with strange texts
and vexed edits
the whiskey dark
can't hide it
it's never dark enough
I keep telling myself to think
but I just go think think
which isn't thinking

So I post up
on the porch
by the ever-smoldering
ashtray
clamp in the earbuds
scan the ether
for audioceuticals
Alabama ragas
skronk and howl
Lil' Weezy

I allow myself
fifteen breaths
per minute
study the angle
of the dog's ears
for signs
of things to come
chart the flightpaths
of humming birds
and fig beetles

but what I started out
to tell you is
I'm drowning
at the liquor store
there's nothing left to do
but assign blame
and turns out
this is all me
and furthermore
the cavalry isn't coming

no more waiting
for the fever to break
it's time
for frontier medicine
right after this cigarette
I will build a proper fence

I will make better mistakes
be courteous
and receptive to courtesy
get my shit straight

I will vibrate
in time and in tune
it's late
but it's not never
and glory glory hallelujah
when I lay my bourbon down
can't you just see it

everyone claps
on one and three
and the black-throated sparrows
serenade me
on the porch
and everything I touch
turns to dopamine

This is Not a Cry For Help

deep in the dog days and I'm all id
and the id says kill fuck eat
I ride a mad horse
I'm driven by errant desire
I don't mean
I want to play slap and tickle
with Suburban Sue
or stand naked in a circle
under a summer moon
and burn pictures of myself
from Jr. High School
I mean I want to fuck shit up
I want to be self-destructive
and still be loved
I want undercooked steak
unplugged blues
unfiltered cigarettes
and uncut bourbon
I want a morphine lollipop
with cocaine sprinkles
I want some bareknuckle
working class sex
I want a lapdance skidmark
If you're going to do a job
do a job

deep in the dog days
and the light
is immoderate and unlovely
my garden
is a fetid place
tomato vines wither
June bugs rot
the birds have forgotten
all but their ugliest songs
the hour of tender beginnings
has passed
it's degeneration time
and God I love to watch
I eat only bird-pecked fruit
start with the bad spots
my wife is ashen at the prospect
of the neighborhood block party
says she thinks I have
a checkered future
I tell her
no one likes
her mix tapes
as much as she does
they lack spiritual depth
and emotional refinement

deep in the dog days
and I'm seeking
inappropriate intimacy
I've been asking strange women
for a hit off their cigarette
at the Covina Farmer's Market
a big blonde in a
watermelon red tube top
let me have one
it was menthol
exhilarating
she had week-old bruises
on her doughy arms
and looked to be running
a low-grade fever
I took a second hit
and stared openly at her breasts
studied them like glowing altarpieces
she reached out
touched my hair
told me my heart was full
of love
I told her I was
the favorite child
of a favorite child

Summer Dress (The Wendrika Poems)

Reasons My Wife Was Crying

For Wendrika
April 4, 1970 to
February 19, 2018

because
Brenda told her how
when she was a little girl
her mother dropped her off
at the bus stop and said
when the bus comes
don't get on it

because Judah Bauer is the best
goddamn guitar player
ever to bend a string
and nobody
wants to talk about it

because
everything is so loud

because
it's too quiet

because
the sky
the sky

because
who died and made you king

because
the days line up
like dominoes

because
all the hopeful Aprils
arriving just in time
on swept back wings

because
a dozen dead cats

because
gay penguins

because
I fed a pork sausage
to a pig
at Sunset Junction

because
she caught me watching her
dancing alone
in a darkened kitchen
humming the Velvet Underground's
"Beginning to See the Light"

because
that one poem
by what's-her-name

because
I offered to help her
find her marbles

because
I let those girls
splash around
in the shallow end
of my heart

because
she missed my mom
more than
she missed her mom

because
she dreamed
of something yellow
swallowing her whole

because
and I quote
you're emotionally distraught
and it scares me

because
sometimes she didn't know
what to do
with her hands

because
she remembered
what grace felt like
it felt like privilege

because
she was going through
final edits
trying to get it all
just right
and it was hard work

because
I love you guys too
just ... fuck

because
grandkid
blanket fort
picnics

because
I made her
that little sculpture thing

because
Sue gave her
a rhinestone tiara

because
Tyler winked at her

because
Ashley's laughter

because
Murray's hugs

because
Jennifer dug that frog
she gave her

because
Tina died too soon

because
Eddie died too soon

because
I told her
I was going to
write a poem called
Reasons My Wife Is Crying

Where Are You?

How was your day?
Are you finding it easier to breathe?
How's your breathing?
Do you ever follow your breath?
Do you have any easy mornings?
Any gravy days?
Do you cry in broad daylight?
Laugh in the dark?
Who do you root for?
What do you rail against?
What are your green eyes full of?

How did you let it slip through your hands?
How?

Are you enchanted?
Disenchanted?
Do you still face dark seductions?
Do you give in just for the dark of it?
Do you have pink light just before sundown?
Are there jacarandas there?
Poppies?
How do you know when it's Spring?
Do you ever pick up feathers?
Do you look at them?
For a long time?

Do you wash your hands?

Are you doing without?
Does anyone have your back?
Your heart?
Do you know any old guys that still ride skateboards?
Does anyone tell you to hold very still?
Do you have any idea what time it is?
Ever?
Did you find the lock of my hair in your pocket?
Did you keep it?
Did you regard it as rare and fine?
Do you ever get to dance?
Are you free?
Have you agency?
Have you dominion?
Over anything?
Have you wonder?
Do you wander?
Wade?
Saunter?
Stroll?
Do you have good shoes?
Are you cold?
Hungry?
Do you have cigarettes?

Will you please call me?

Best Western Parking Lot,
San Dimas, California

I can never unrip
your favorite shirt
off of you
if I could
I might not

we were so young
the clouds were moving
West to East
and you looked
punk rock

feral
quaking
in your
red bra
and messy makeup

Denuded

her dress
was a wind-driven
late-season wildfire
her breasts
only forty percent contained

the heat was sinful
the fire raged
through dense thickets
areas that hadn't burned
for ages

let it smolder
she said
work at the flanks
let devil winds
have my canyons

let tongue
of flame
stoke my core
scorch my flora
scatter my fauna

let it burn
let it hurt me
let it reduce me
to ash
alkaline and anodyne

Interrogative Mode

How old were you?
What were you wearing?
Did hot tears well up
    in your eyes?
Spill down your cheeks?
Did endorphins flood your system?
Did you feel the foundation buckle?
Did your hair tangle beautifully
    around your eyes
    and against your lips?
Was it sharp?
The blade honed thin and terrible?
Did you take the grown-up dose?
Did your mind rejoin your body
    when it was safe to do so?
Did your eyes change color
    every few minutes?
Did you love it like nicotine?
Did it leave stretchmarks on your heart?
Was it fun out of the gate?
Did you yearn for the bite of the whip
    as you entered the homestretch?

How old were you?
What were you wearing?
Did you wink and drain your glass?
Did it come in waves?
Were there varieties of darkness?
Did your fire keep the wolves at bay?
Did it light up the night sky?
For a hundred miles?
Were you subjected to the gaze?
Of poetry?
Itself?
Did you taste all the poems
        ever breathed into your mouth?
Did you pray as hard as an atheist could?
Were there territories of yourself
        that you kept in reserve?
Was your beauty a curse?
Did it tickle your ass?
Did you finger every bud
        in the bag?
Were you fully vested with wonder?
With glory?
Did you ponder it for a year?
Another year?
The rest of your life?

How old were you?
What were you wearing?
What did it feel like?
The grass under your feet?
The sun on your face?
A call to prayer?
A call to arms?
A clusterfuck?
Like myopia?
Fairydust?
Snake handling?
Dinner bell?
Check out time?
Search party?
Hex?
Incantation?
Like sitting in the shade with friends,
    for fuck's sake?
Like a red house over yonder?
A pair of binoculars flipped backwards?
A tan line on your ring finger?
A Virgin of Guadalupe shaped
    water stain above your bed?
Ten thousand roses and a tangle
    of thorns?
Like the sound of something
    beginning to crack?

How old were you?
What were you wearing?
Did it come out of nowhere?
Like a barfight?
Swift and mighty?
Were you barefoot?
With cigarettes?
What time was it?
The moon?
What phase?
Lipstick?
Or no?
Did you push hard?
Was there pushback?
Were you running from
      or running toward?
Was every door an exit?
Were you able to just get up
      and walk out?
Did you have to squirm free?
Are the clawmarks atrocious?

Zazen

it's a hundred and stupid
in the SGV

under a white blue
daytime moon

in an overexposed
August sky

wearing only a backwards
Circle Jerks trucker hat

hair freshly washed
toenails painted lotus white

she sits on the lawn
criss cross applesauce

finds her breath
and follows it

with amazing grace
and half-open eyes

when the sweat trickle
and grass prickle

grow too vexing
she takes breaks

moves to the shade
rolls cigarettes

from a large yellow
can of tobacco

smokes like she'll never die
calm as a burning monk

Summer Dress

she adored the dress
had to have it
problem was
H&M had it
in both plum and pumpkin

holding them out
at arms length
she was sure
she loved one of them
we walked out with both

the orange one
became a closet placeholder
the purple one
grew faded
and butter soft with wear

it's the one I'm holding now
balled up
and pressed to my nose

after everything
broke sideways
and went all shitty

the pristine orange one
went straight into
the Amvets donation box

the purple one
rumpled and unwashed
I stuffed into my duffle

Note

I waited here for you
as long as I could

the elephant in the room
is going to be just fine
the hooks and cattle prods
haven't harmed her
she's already forgotten

I rolled you some cigarettes
before I left

I waited here
as long as I could
scanning the street
certain the very next car
would screech to a stop

and spit you out

Gone (Ghazals)

Blue

Jeannette Bellwood liked her Marlboros red, her
    Sabbath Black and her hiphugger jeans blue.
When she got shipped off to Grandma's house in Reno
    all the Canyon Boys were blue.

Nicely microdosed, the Pitzer hippies drove
    north on Mills Avenue.
KSPC blasted French psychedelia. *Vive la*
    DJ Fifi LaRoux! *Sacre bleu*!

The Queen of Starlite Mobile Estates spun toward him,
    her robe falling open, exposing one breast, and said,
"Listen. Here's the deal. I'm going to drink and
    catch the light and fuck off into the blue."

Weaving down Glendora Mountain Road, podcast
    in his earbuds, he was stoned on joy,
chanting Hare Krishna along with Radhanath Swami
    and Duncan Trussell. Then the tire blew.

Linda Arkansas woke up sunny side down,
    wearing a barbed wire tiara.
She mumbled, "Everything is all fucktangular."
    Her aura was black and blue.

The message was buried deep into the B-side
        of a Maxell C-90 cassette mix tape,
between Jon Spencer Blues Explosion's "Blue Green Olga"
        and Elvis Costello's "Almost Blue."

I could be there soon. Not much to carry
        since the trailer burned down,
since the flames leapt up and the hot winds
        blew and blew.

Indulge me for just a moment. Close your eyes -
        sit up straight, with your shoulders back.
Imagine me rich with story. Imagine me at ease
        in the world. Imagine me without the blues.

Focus

Anything is weird if you stare at it long
    enough. Really focus.
There is a layer of strange in everything. It's
    a matter of focus.

Silk chafing like chainmail, Mrs. Langdon took the
    garden shears and cut
off the tender nipples of her breasts. They were
    occluding her focus.

"This is not a drill. You be indfidel eyes. You be
    the scent of possibility.
You're the wink of the complicit. You're
    hydraulic surprise. People, focus!"

Julie ran away to Venice Beach and changed her
    name to Patchouli. Now she has
armpit dreads, a "Vegan Girls Don't Swallow" tattoo
    and her eyes are all out of focus.

Wild-eyed, sweat-drenched and whiskey-sodden.
    Midnight meltdown in 29 Palms.
They could hear the vultures on the roof. Fresh bottle.
    Full moon focus.

Allowing for unlimited states of mind, Polly Centric
     packs a bag for her
weekend at the Zen Center, leaving room to carry
     home all her extra focus.

"Yes, King Daddy, oh hell yes. It's like when
     I spin around
and around and everything blurs, but my body
     stays in focus."

Open

You know so much already. The lushery and lechery.
    The brilliant way it opens.
How it's heavy and delicate at once. The short, sharp
    blows. The blinds pried open.

Repitition dulls my fear, but for three nights
    running, knowing no Latin,
she has cried out "*noli me tángere*" in her sleep.
    Her eyes wide open.

She doesn't weigh words, doesn't finesse the
    message. Spins jagged fables,
just lets it fly. She's salty and juicy and she
    kisses with her mouth open.

It ain't rocket surgery. After correcting for
    whiskey-wobble, her moral compass
always points south. She's three-thirds easy
    and the playground is open.

The sun has set and the rules have changed.
    See the happy yokemates,
their hair knotted into a single whip.
    She unlocks the door, he sweeps it open.

Our lies are always wishes. Clothing is a lie.
    Naked, we glisten with truth.
Every twitch and wiggle is disclosure. Look at
    us, so honest, so open.

My appetites are manifold and voracious. I am
    starving ego and obvious need.
Yes, this is hunger in my eyes.
    This is as far as my arms open.

Gone

11:08 PM. Three inch stack of Pringles, cup of
    this morning's coffee gone
cold, fold-over PB&J. This is what dinner looks
    like with her gone.

Nothing is ever just one thing. Nothing is fixed.
    Nothing immutable.
True love, good dog, sandstone bluff; wind, water
    time – gone.

Liquor, that liar, has deceived you and lust has
    perverted your heart.
I've a good mind to rouge my nipples and
    hit the road. Get fucking gone.

Existence is a continuum. We are present,
    future, future perfect, imperfect,
pluperfect and past. We are plenum and vacuum. We
    are gone and here and gone.

Wearing only panties and a Santa hat on a
    strangely warm December day,
she sits on the porch smoking. Mumbling curses.
    Looking somewhat gone.

Sweaty roughhouse and carnal sob. A hovering sense
    of guilt, no bigger than
a small headache. On cue, the radio bleats,
    "Gone Daddy gone, the love is gone."

A raven circles, lands on her shoulder and leans
    in to whisper in her ear.
Her breath catches in her throat, but she
    doesn't cry out. The conclusion was foregone.

About the Author

King Daddy is a father, grandfather, and bookworm. He dabbles in nudism and Buddhism, revels in primitive acoustic blues and seeks to dwell in the now. He is a life-long resident of the San Gabriel Valley. He sometimes writes poems in black notebooks and has been a member of the performance poetry troupe, Poets in Distress, since the days when pot had seeds. He has won no literary awards or prizes.

BAMBOO DART PRESS

112 N. Harvard Ave. #65
Claremont, CA 91711

chapbooks@bamboodartpress.com
www.bamboodartpress.com

www.ingramcontent.com/pod-product-compliance
Lightning Source LLC
Chambersburg PA
CBHW081642040426
42449CB00015B/3426